BOB DYLAN

Christmas In The Heart

AMSCO PUBLICATIONS
a Part of The Music Sales Group
New York/London/Paris/Sydney/Copenhagen/Berlin/Tokyo/Madrid

All of Bob Dylan's U.S. royalties from the sales of "Christmas In The Heart"
will be donated to Feeding America (feedingamerica.org).

All of Bob Dylan's international royalties from the sales of "Christmas In The Heart"
will be donated to Crisis (crisis.org.uk) and the World Food Programme (wfp.org).

Cover design: Coco Shinomiya
Front cover: © VisualLanguage.com
Inside Photo © Leonard Freed/MagnumPhotos
Back Cover Illustration by Edwin Fotheringham
Arrangements for publication by David Pearl
Project Editor: David Bradley

This book © 2009 by Amsco Publications,
A Division of Music Sales Corporation, New York

Order No. AM 999185
ISBN: 978-0-8256-3730-8
HL Item Number: 14037461

Exclusive Distributor for the United States, Canada, Mexico and U.S. possessions:
Hal Leonard Corporation
7777 West Bluemound Road, Milwaukee, WI 53213 USA

Exclusive Distributors for the rest of the World:
Music Sales Limited
14-15 Berners Street, London W1T 3LJ England
Music Sales Pty. Limited
20 Resolution Drive, Caringbah, NSW 2229, Australia

Printed in the United States of America

HERE COMES SANTA CLAUS

Words and Music by Gene Autry and Oakley Haldeman

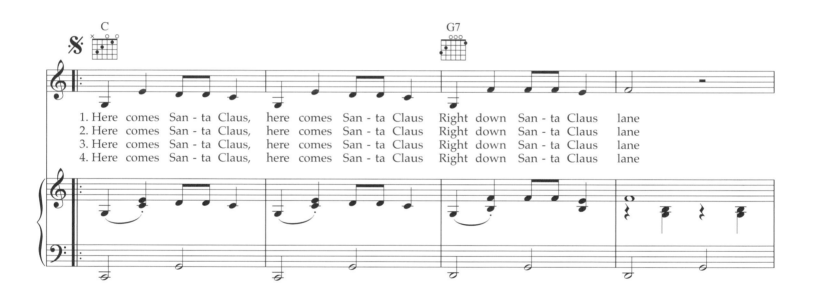

1. Here comes San - ta Claus, here comes San - ta Claus Right down San - ta Claus lane
2. Here comes San - ta Claus, here comes San - ta Claus Right down San - ta Claus lane
3. Here comes San - ta Claus, here comes San - ta Claus Right down San - ta Claus lane
4. Here comes San - ta Claus, here comes San - ta Claus Right down San - ta Claus lane

Vix - en and Blitz - en and all his rein - deer Pul - lin' on the reins
He's got a bag that is filled with toys For the boys and girls a - gain
He does - n't care if you're rich or poor For he loves you just the same
He'll come a - round when the chimes ring out When it's Christ - mas morn a - gain

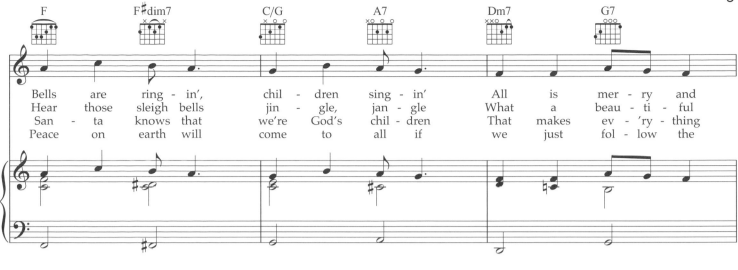

Bells are ring - in', chil - dren sing - in' All is mer - ry and
Hear those sleigh bells jin - gle, jan - gle What a beau - ti - ful
San - ta knows that we're God's chil - dren That makes ev - 'ry - thing
Peace on earth will come to all if we just fol - low the

bright Hang your stock - ings, say your pray'rs 'Cause
sight Jump in bed, cov - er your head 'Cause
right Fill your hearts with a Christ - mas cheer 'Cause
light So fill your hearts with a Christ - mas cheer 'Cause

To Coda ⊕ | 1., 2. | 3. | *D.S. al Coda*

San - ta Claus comes to - night! night!

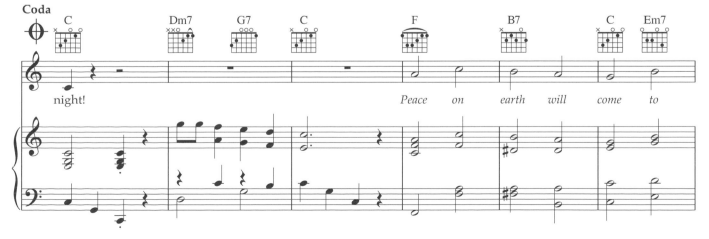

Coda

night! *Peace on earth will come to*

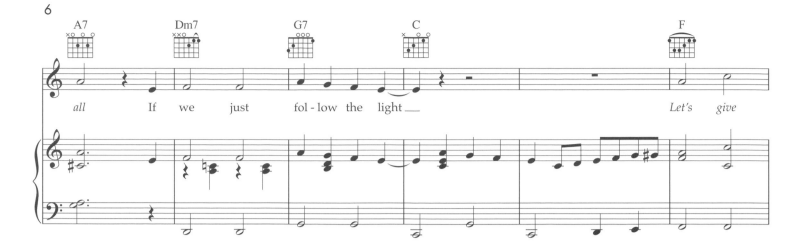

all If we just fol-low the light ___ Let's give

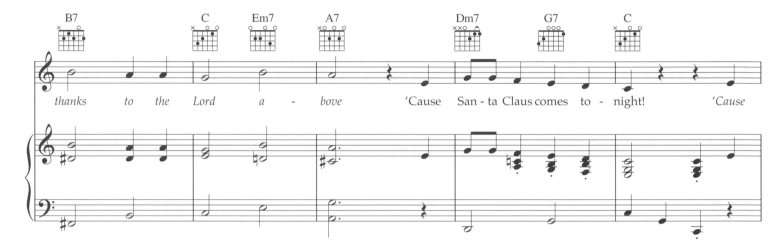

thanks to the Lord a - bove 'Cause San - ta Claus comes to - night! 'Cause

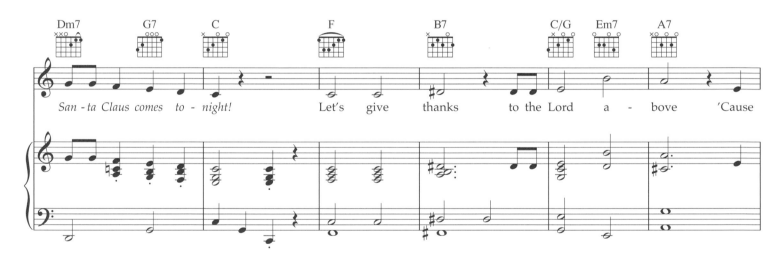

San - ta Claus comes to - night! Let's give thanks to the Lord a - bove 'Cause

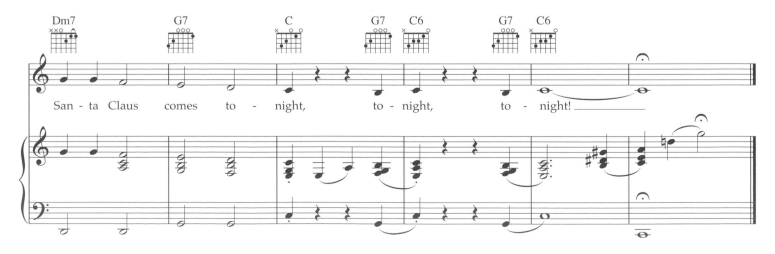

San - ta Claus comes to - night, to - night, to - night! ___

DO YOU HEAR WHAT I HEAR?

Words and Music by Noel Regney and Gloria Shayne

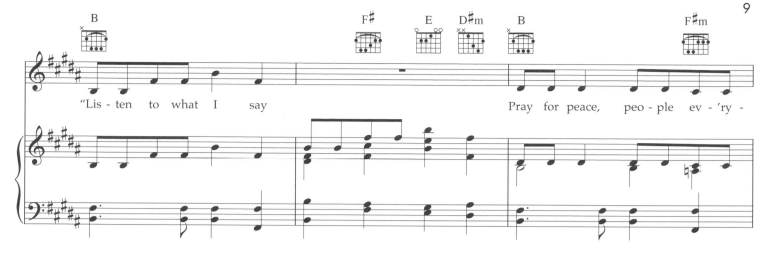

"Lis - ten to what I say   Pray for peace, peo - ple ev - 'ry -

where   Lis - ten to what I say,   A child,   a child,

sleep - ing in the night He will bring us good - ness and light   He will bring   us

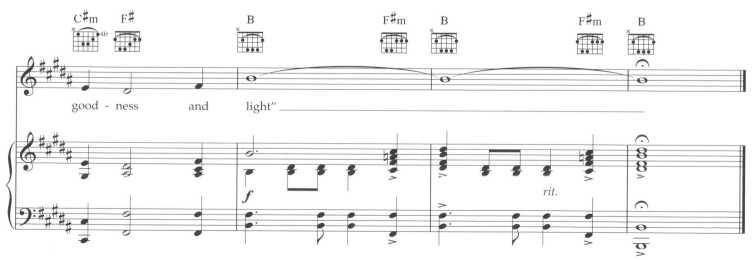

good - ness   and   light" _____

WINTER WONDERLAND

Words by Dick Smith   Music by Felix Bernard

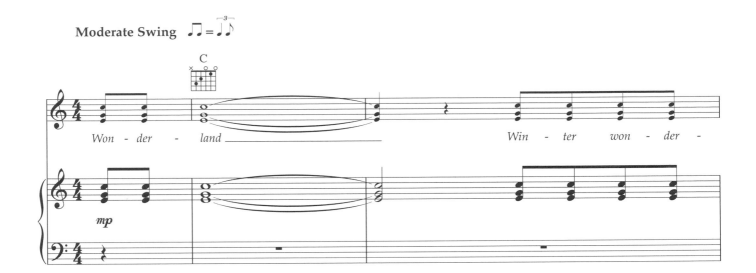

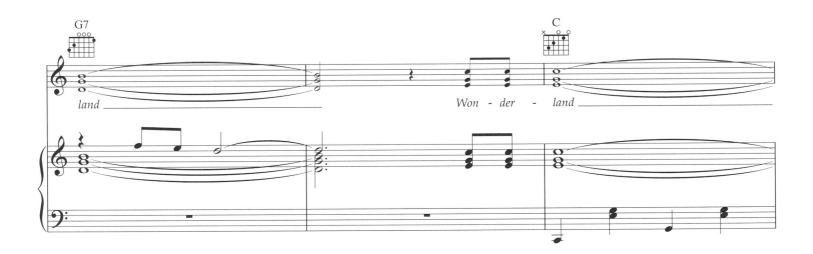

12

HARK THE HERALD ANGELS SING

Traditional, Arranged by Bob Dylan

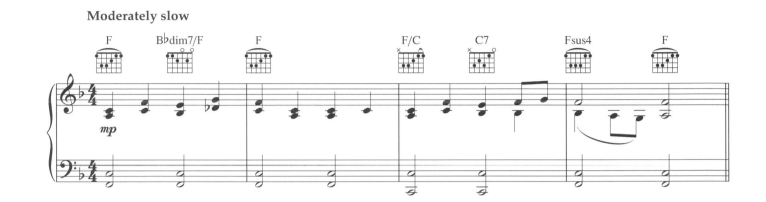

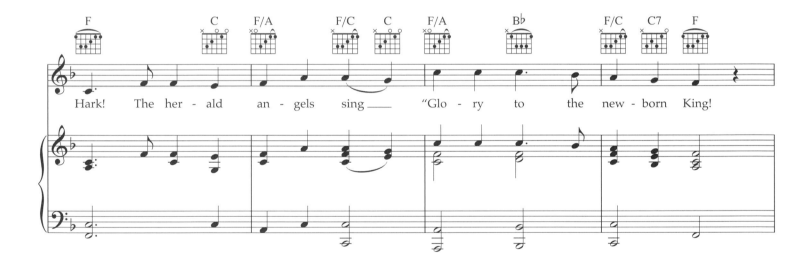

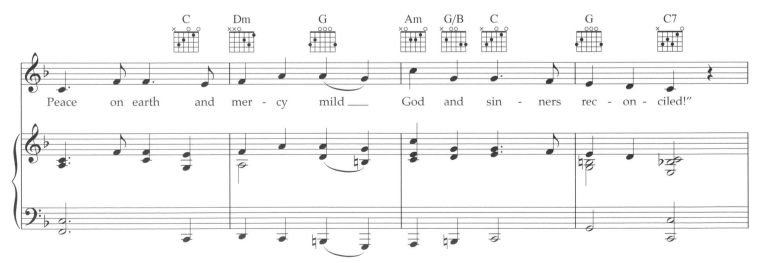

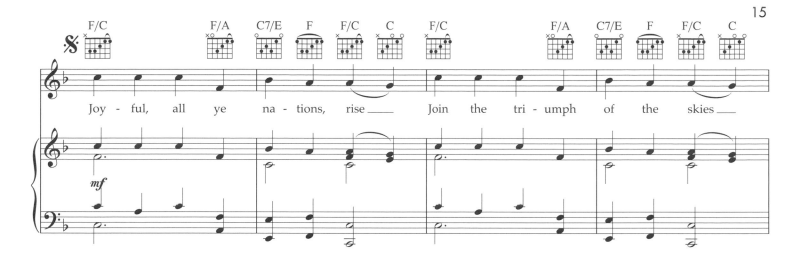

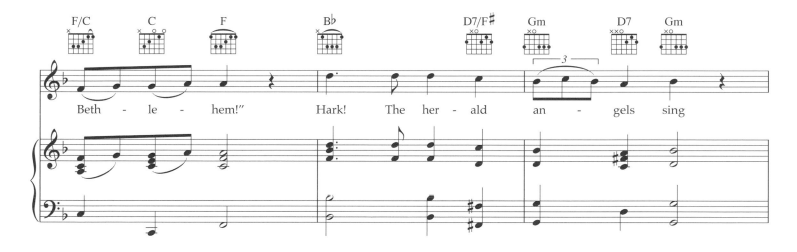

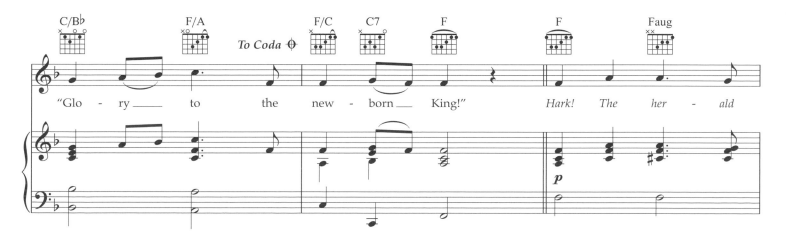

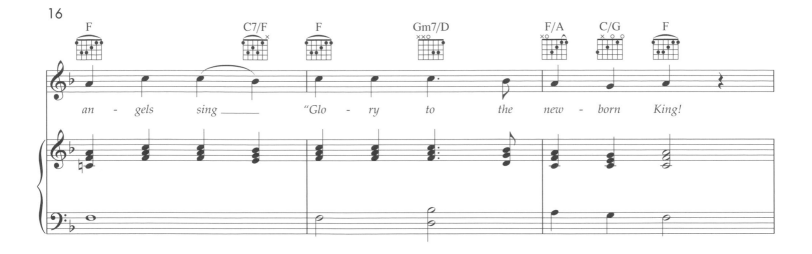

an - gels sing _____ "Glo - ry to the new - born King!

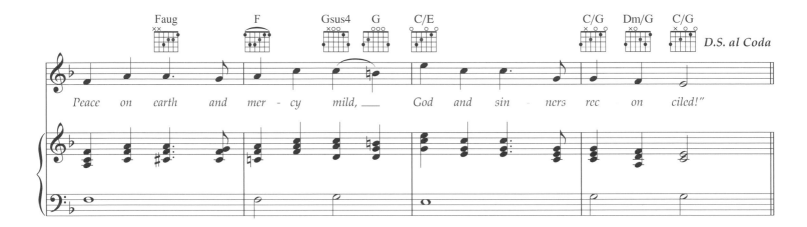

Peace on earth and mer - cy mild, ___ God and sin - ners rec - on - ciled!"

D.S. al Coda

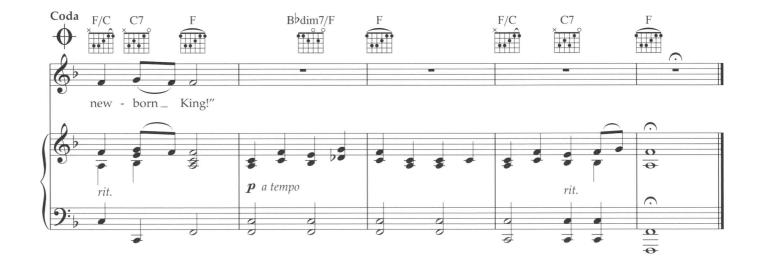

Coda

new - born _ King!"

rit.   p a tempo   rit.

I'LL BE HOME FOR CHRISTMAS

Words and Music by Kim Gannon and Walter Kent

Slowly, in 2

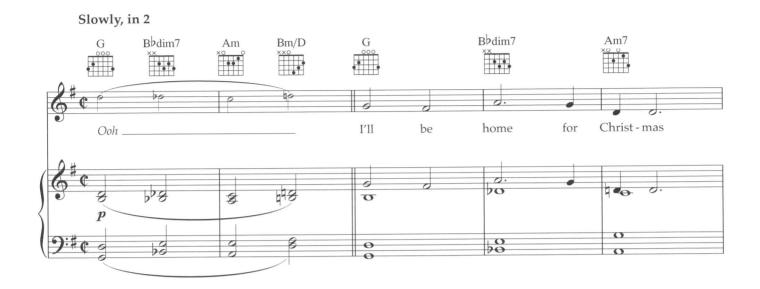

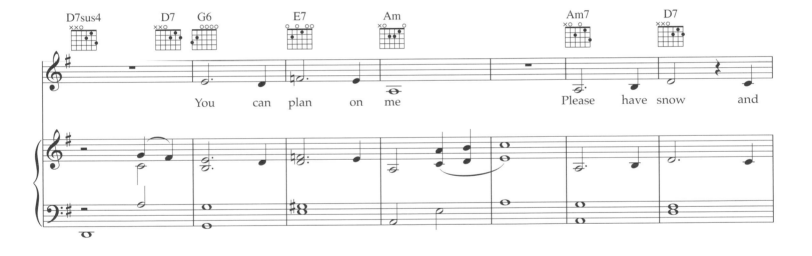

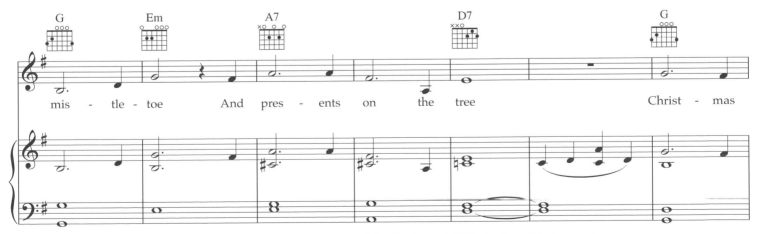

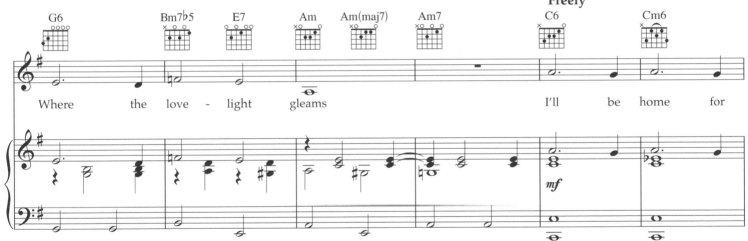

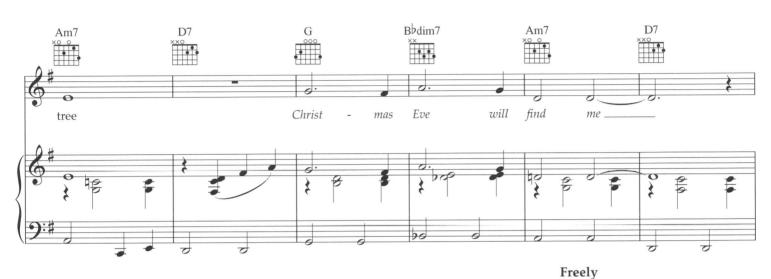

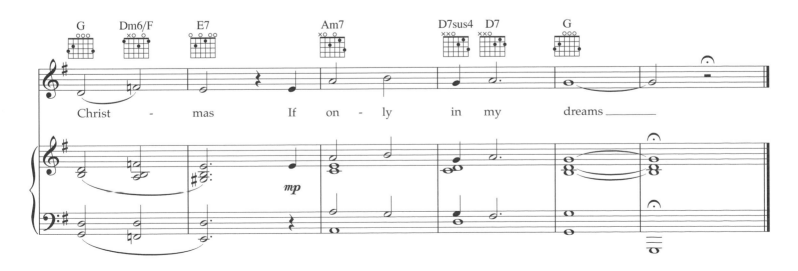

LITTLE DRUMMER BOY

Words and Music by Harry Simeone, Henry Onorati and Katherine Davis

21

That's fit to give a King, pa rum pum pum pum, rum pum pum pum,

rum pum pum pum

Shall I play for you, pa rum pum pum pum

On __ my drum?

Mar - y nod - ded, pa rum pum pum pum

The ox and lamb kept time, pa rum pum pum pum

I played my drum for Him, pa

THE CHRISTMAS BLUES

Words and Music by Sammy Cahn and David Holt

26

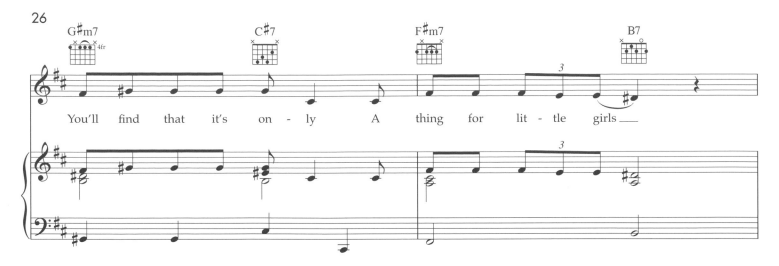

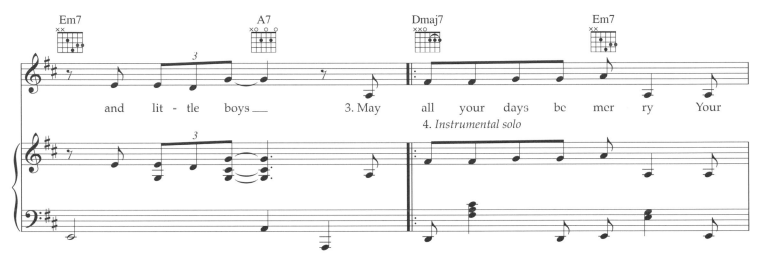

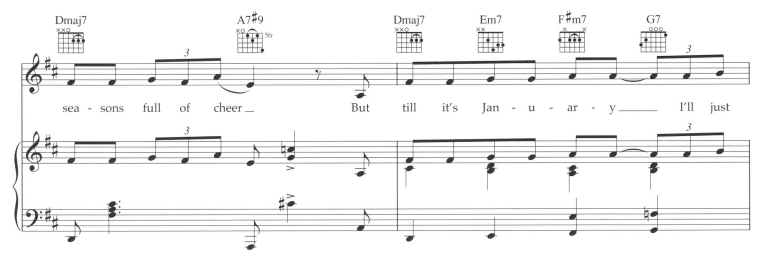

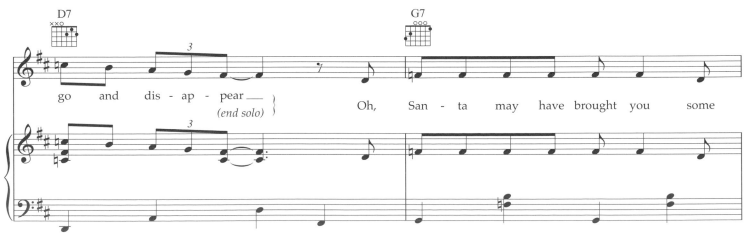

HAVE YOURSELF A MERRY LITTLE CHRISTMAS

Words and Music by Hugh Martin and Ralph Blane

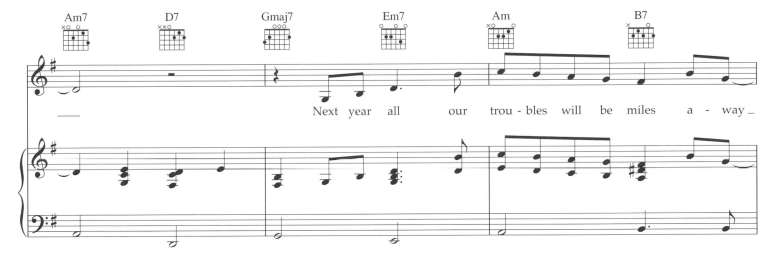

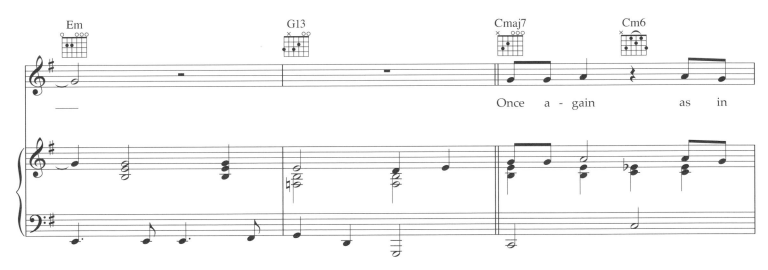

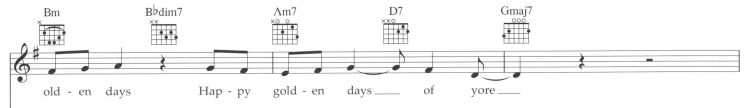

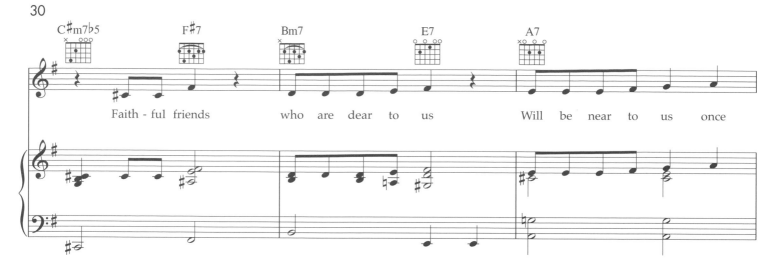

Faith - ful friends who are dear to us Will be near to us once

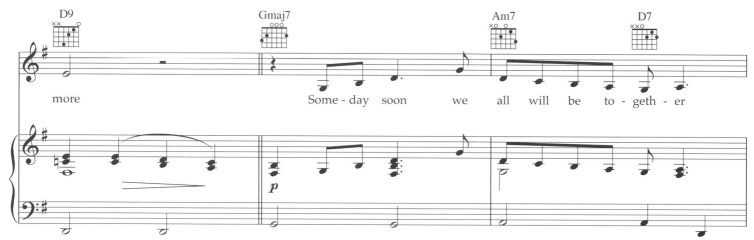

more Some - day soon we all will be to - geth - er

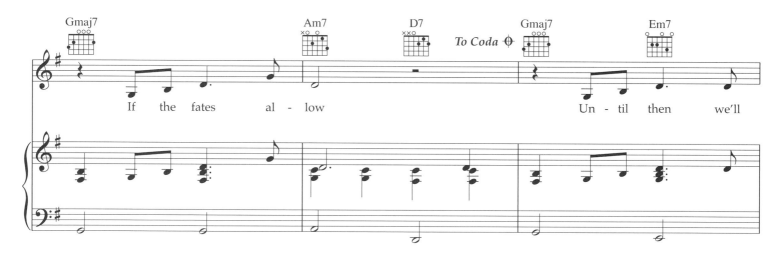

If the fates al - low *To Coda* Un - til then we'll

have to mo - tor through some - how So

MUST BE SANTA

Words and Music by Hal Moore and William Fredericks

Fast, in 2

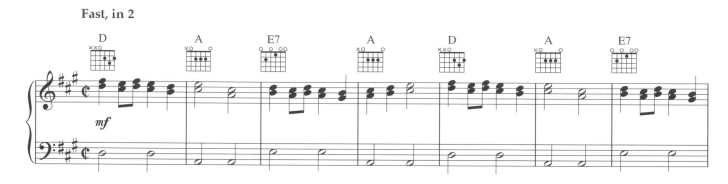

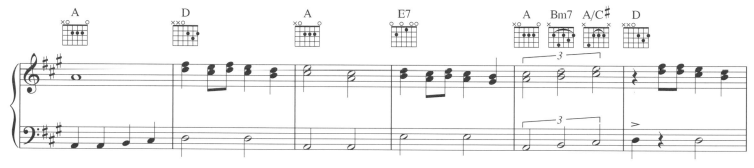

1. Who's got a beard that's long and white?
2. Who wears boots and a suit of red?
3. Who's got a big red cher-ry nose?

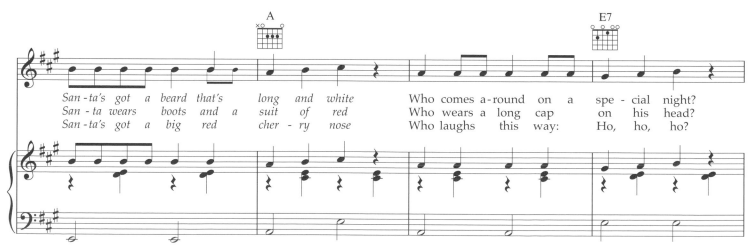

San-ta's got a beard that's long and white   Who comes a-round on a spe-cial night?
San-ta wears boots and a suit of red   Who wears a long cap on his head?
San-ta's got a big red cher-ry nose   Who laughs this way: Ho, ho, ho?

San - ta Claus

3.
Cap on head   Suit that's red   Spe - cial night   Beard that's white   Must be San - ta

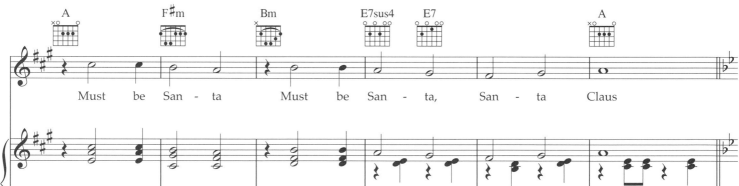

Must be San - ta   Must be San - ta, San - ta Claus

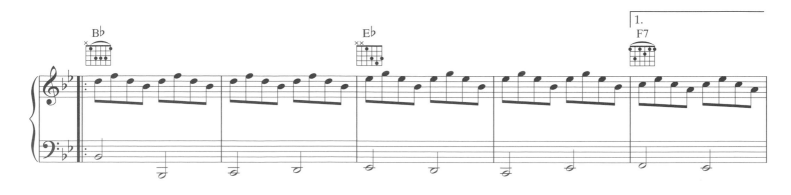

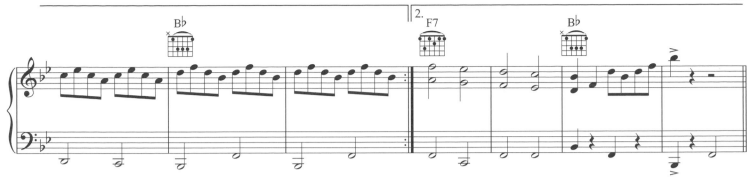

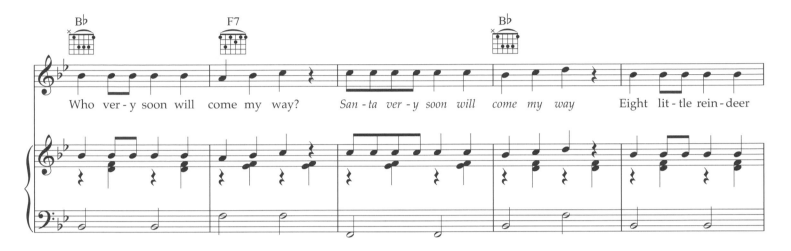

Who ver-y soon will come my way? *San-ta ver-y soon will come my way* Eight lit-tle rein-deer

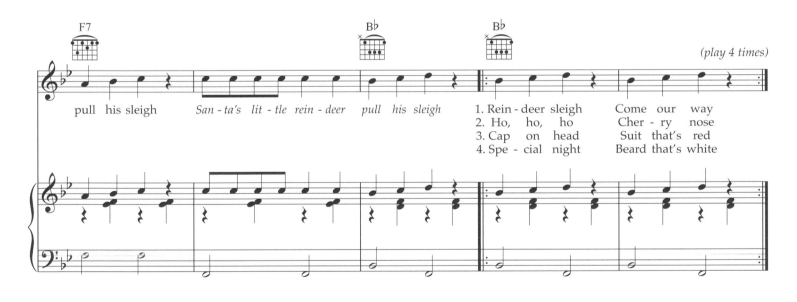

pull his sleigh *San-ta's lit-tle rein-deer pull his sleigh*

(play 4 times)

1. Rein-deer sleigh   Come our way
2. Ho, ho, ho   Cher-ry nose
3. Cap on head   Suit that's red
4. Spe-cial night   Beard that's white

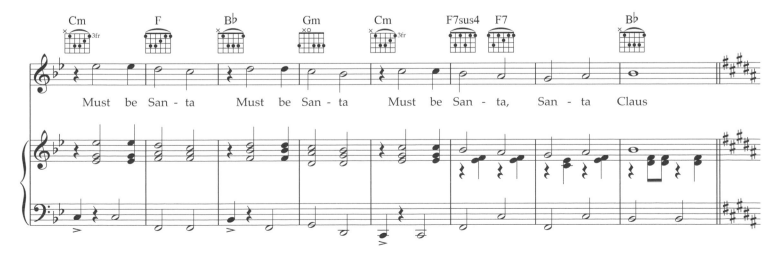

Must be San-ta   Must be San-ta   Must be San-ta, San-ta Claus

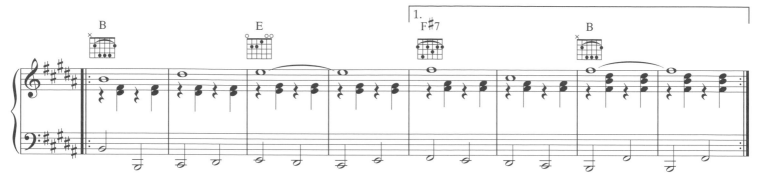

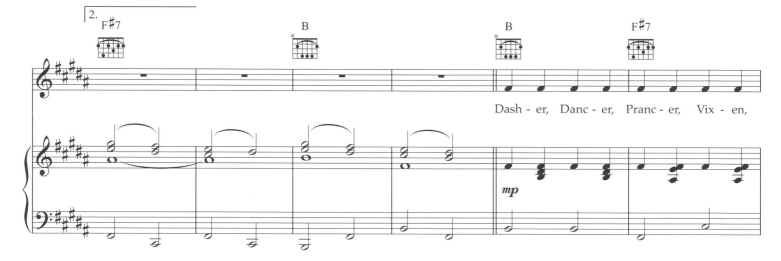

Dash - er, Danc - er, Pranc - er, Vix - en,

Ei - sen - how - er, Ken - ne - dy, John - son, Nix - on Dash - er, Danc - er, Pranc - er, Vix - en, Car - ter, Rea - gan,

Bush and Clin - ton 1. Rein - deer sleigh Come our way Must be San - ta Must be
2. Ho, ho, ho Cher - ry nose
3. Cap on head Suit that's red
4. Spe - cial night Beard that's white

(play 4 times)

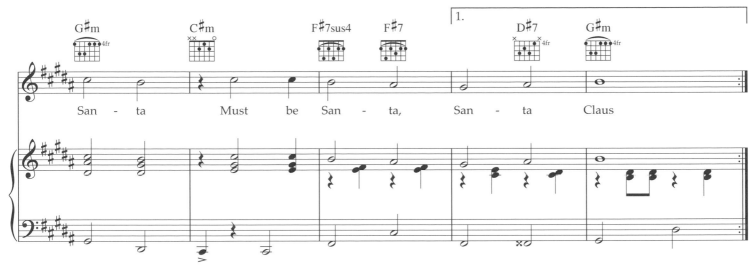

Santa   Must   be   San - ta,   San - ta   Claus

San - ta   Claus

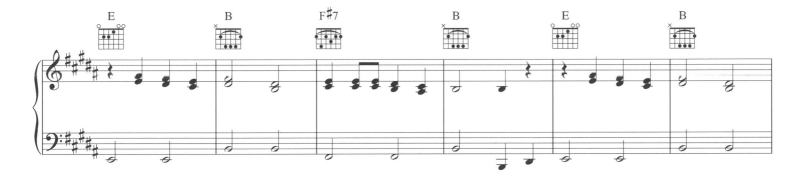

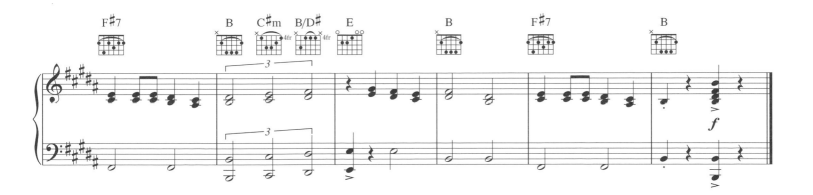

O' COME ALL YE FAITHFUL (ADESTE FIDELES)

Traditional, Arranged by Bob Dylan

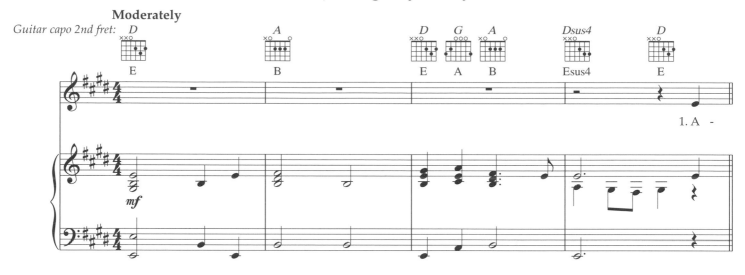

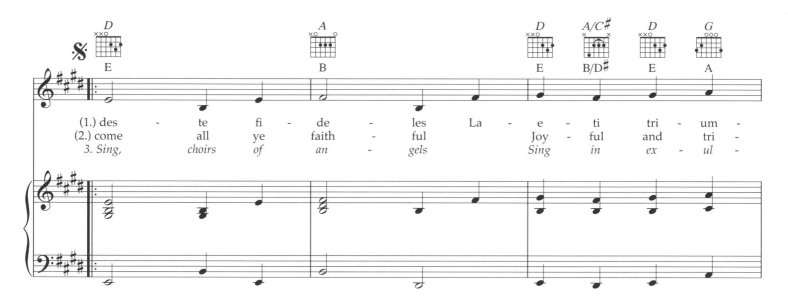

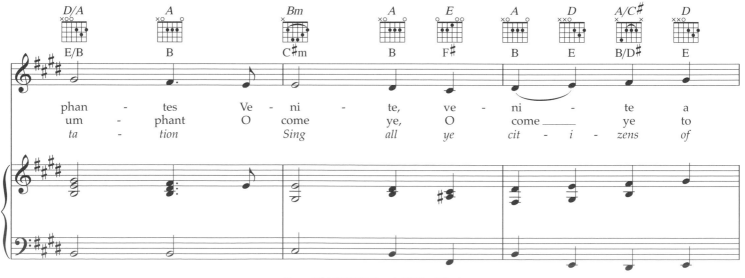

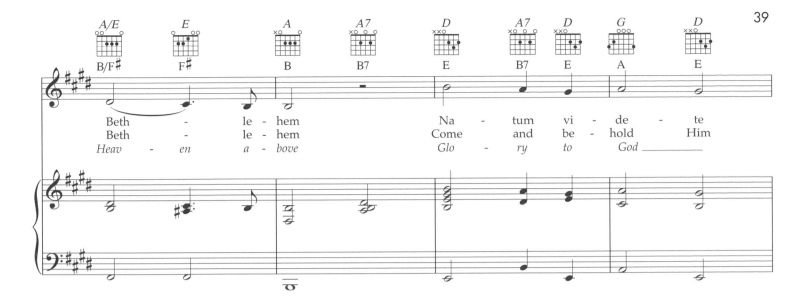

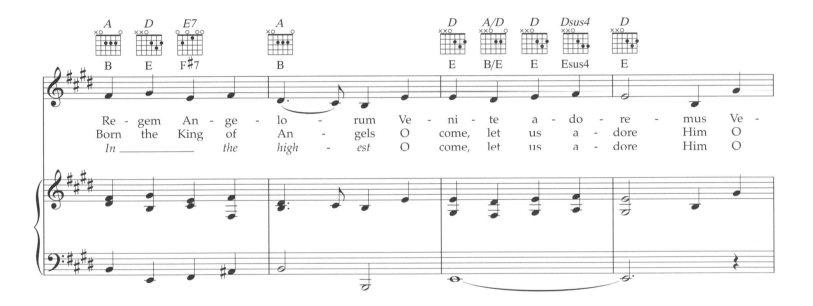

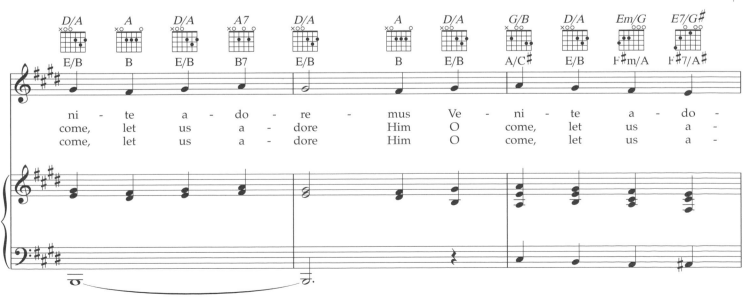

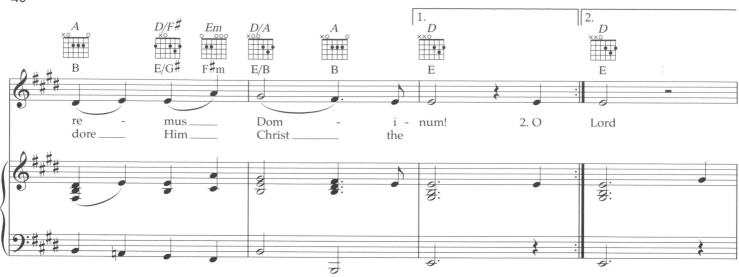

re -   mus____ Dom - i - num!   2. O   Lord
dore ____ Him ____ Christ ____   the

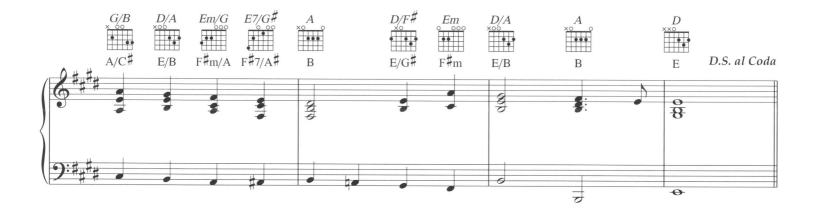

D.S. al Coda

Slowly

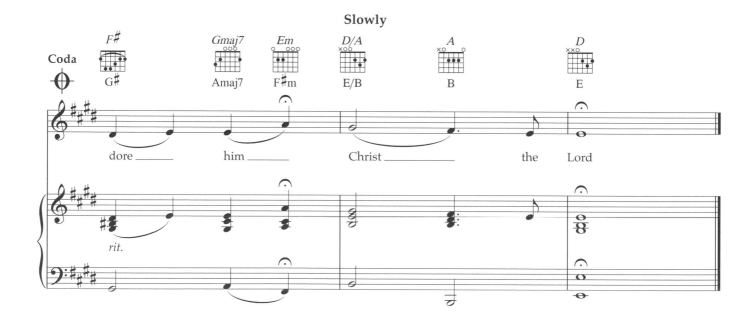

dore ____ him ____ Christ ____ the   Lord

rit.

SILVER BELLS

Words and Music by Jay Livingston and Ray Evans

42

THE FIRST NOEL

Traditional, Arranged by Bob Dylan

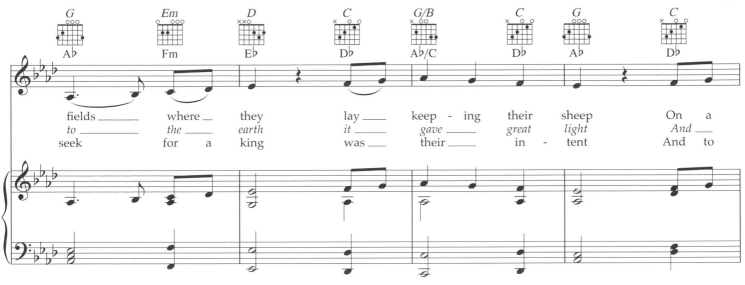

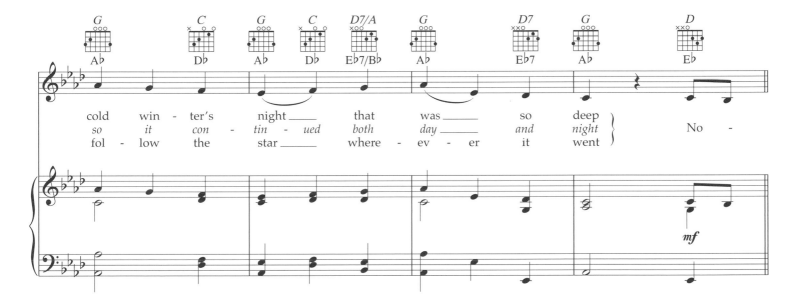

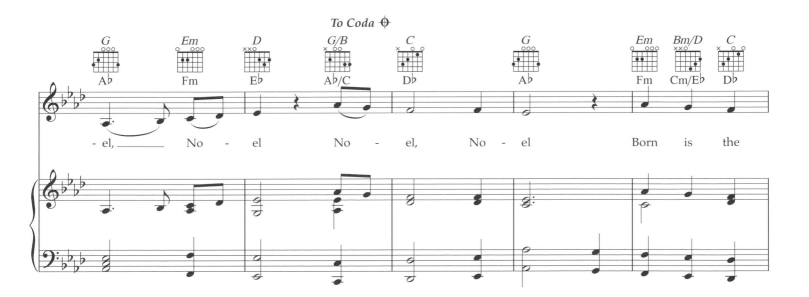

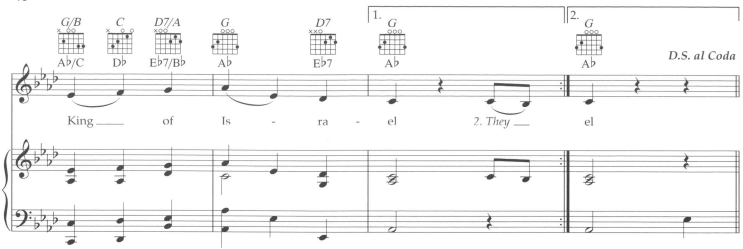

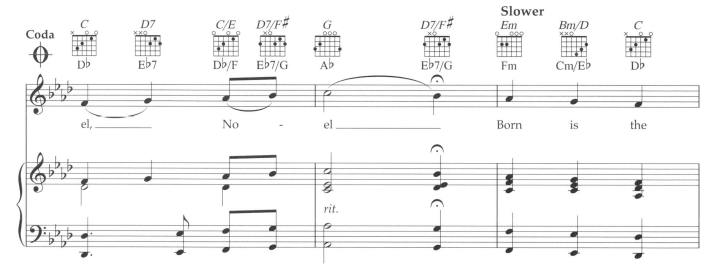

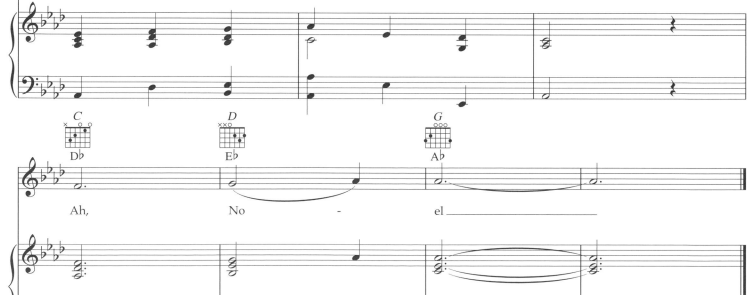

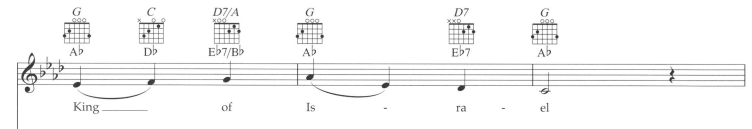

CHRISTMAS ISLAND

Words and Music by Lyle Moraine

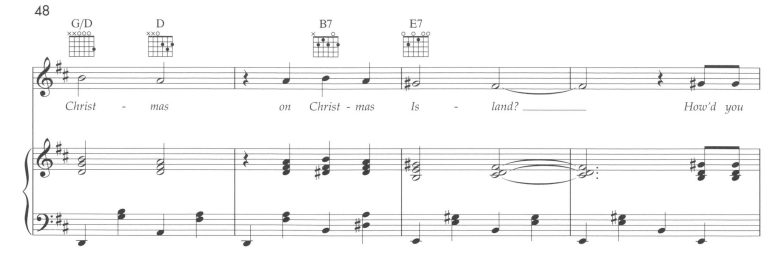

Christ - mas on Christ - mas Is - land? _____ How'd you

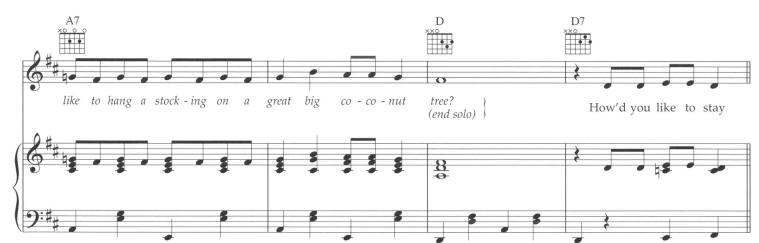

like to hang a stock - ing on a great big co - co - nut tree?
(end solo)

How'd you like to stay

up late _ like the is - land - ers do? Wait for San - ta to

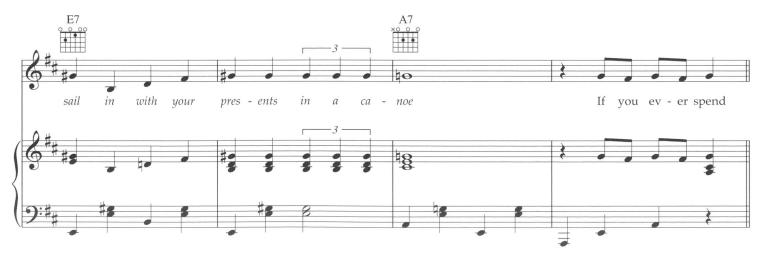

sail in with your pres - ents in a ca - noe If you ev - er spend

THE CHRISTMAS SONG

Music and Lyric by Mel Tormé and Robert Wells

51

52

O' LITTLE TOWN OF BETHLEHEM

Traditional, Arranged by Bob Dylan

bless - ings of all His heav'n No ear may hear His com - - ing But

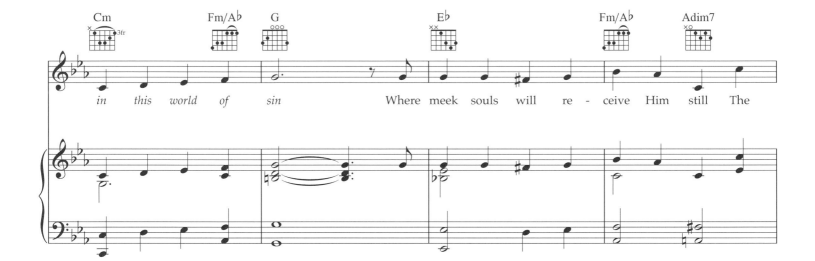

in this world of sin Where meek souls will re - ceive Him still The

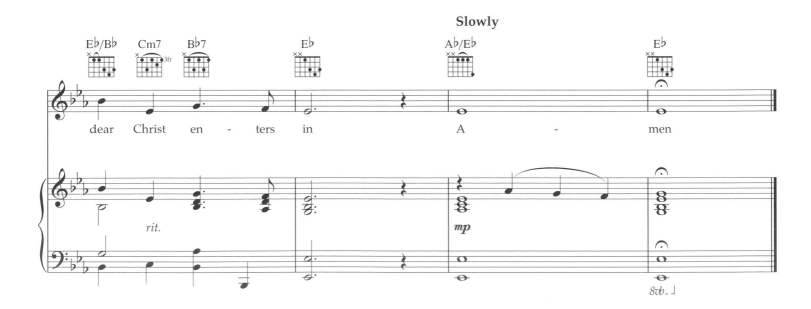

dear Christ en - ters in A - men

rit.

Slowly

mp

8vb